Passion, Purpose, and Principles

Passion, Purpose, and Principles

*A Beautiful Life Is
The One With A Purpose*

Find Yours

Sharon Sydney Miranda

To order additional copies of this book, contact:
Xlibris Corporation
0-800-644-6988
www.xlibrispublishing.co.uk
Orders@xlibrispublishing.co.uk
301544

Contents

Dedication

This book is dedicated to my family . . . Look what the Lord has done! Wow!

In the midst of all darkness, there is always light at the end of the tunnel. The principle is to "Never Quit"

Father God, please have Your way with this book in Jesus Name Amen.

Acknowledgements

I am just amazed once again at this point in time. I cannot believe I am writing yet another book. This is awesome!

I would like to start by thanking the Almighty God for saving my soul. Thank you so much for the talents, gifts, blessings and opportunities given to me to live a purpose driven life. Thanks once again for the direction and the strength that keeps me going every single day.

Let me take this opportunity to thank the Senior Pastor of Kings Way International Christian Centre (KICC) Mathew Ashmolowo and his wife Yemisi Ashmolowo. Thanks so much for your great preaching and all the inspiring messages.

Another thank you to Pastor Dipo Oluyomi you are such a great Dad to us. (your daughters from Uganda)

Many thanks to my mentor and mother in the Lord Dr Josephine Kyambadde, Truly you are a virtuous woman of God. Your support and love is priceless! You are the real deal! We need more people like you who can discover our dreams, talents and gifts and nurture them to flourish. Thank you for forwarding my book. God bless you mum.

To Pastor Daniel Marley of Miracle of Faith International Ministries and Pastor David Ssenfuma of Source Of Life Church Uganda. You are such great leaders. Thanks so much for your support, encouragement and prayers.

Next, a huge thank you to my mentor and CEO of Action Wealth Group of Companies Geoffrey Semaganda. You introduced me to the reality of the business world and you have been such an inspiration. Your teachings and philosophies are awesome. Thanks for all your on-going support. You have enabled me to develop and grow not just as a speaker but also as an entrepreneur. You have been a huge blessing to our team at Wealth Magnets Company. God bless you.

My gratitude goes to my mentors Mr and Mrs Godfrey Sekisonge. It is amazing how you showed up on the scene and great opportunities came forth. I am grateful for all your love and support.

Another big thank you to Mr Jackson Luweero; Managing Director of Europolar;-Air Cargo Transport Company. I really appreciate all your support and advice.

Next, a huge thank you to Jessica Birungi; The best Personal Assistant in the world. Girl you are the real deal! Thanks for all your support. God Bless you.

To my friends as well as my brothers in the Lord and my network team; Pr. Peter Nsubuga, Pr. Robert Jr Mukiibi and Richard Babajide. You guys are great. Thank you so much for making things happen. You have done a phenomenal job. God Bless you.

Next, a huge thank you to Gerald Hedlund for all your support on this project. You have done an incredible job. God bless you.

To my friends; Evelyn Blessing, Kiena, Josephine, Phylma, Angie, Connie, Harriet, Tom, Steve, Samuel, and Viola. I love you guys and God Bless you all.

A special thank you to my girlfriend and workout partner Robina Kasozi. You are such a joke! Your commitment and motivation to keep us fit and health is amazing. Many blessings to you.

To my Youth Group in Uganda; Penninah, Jackie, Margret, Olivia, Rachael, Betty, Grace, Gorret, Monix, Mulongo, Ian and Godie. I love you guys.

Finally to all our clients out there, you are amazing and without you, there would be no empowerment workshops and seminars.

Foreword

At the outset of this book, let me take a moment to introduce you to my spiritual daughter Sharon. I have known Sharon for quite some time. She was introduced to me by Pastor David Ssenfuma. (Source Of Life Church)

She is courageous, loving, firm, beautiful, ambitious and graced. Through our mentoring sessions I have always noticed that she is a very intelligent woman of God, stands for prosperity, hungers to see other people prosper too and become successful in their lives. After understanding that the key to achieving success and living a fulfilled life is finding one's purpose, Sharon has written this book to encourage people who have not yet discovered their purpose in life to do so.

Finding your purpose in life is very important. It is where meaning and significance comes from. What is your life driven by? Some people are driven by their past experiences and they spend their whole lives running from that but this prevents them from living and enjoying the present moment. Others are driven by their possessions and the desire to acquire more overwhelms them and they're consumed by that which distracts them from discovering the primary reason to their existence. The starting point is to understand why you were created.

Having a purpose in life will increase your motivation and decrease your frustration. Purpose allows you to focus on what you are here for. It gives you a track to run on.

For us to fulfil our purpose we need to have principles laid down. Principles are the core of what any of us do and we must have passion for our principles. Principles make us better people.

Nothing great is ever attained in life without passion for it. Nothing great is ever affirmed in life without passion. Passion is what rejuvenates life. Passion makes the impossible possible. Passion gives you a reason to get up in the morning and start your day, "I'm going to do the following today." Without zeal and purpose, life becomes boring. It becomes monotonous. It becomes regular. It becomes unexciting.

In this book Sharon imparts some of her wisdom, knowledge, insight and conviction. She encourages people to find their purpose and pursue it until they succeed in life.

It is my pleasure to introduce to you an inspiring and intelligent lady in the land: Sharon Sydney Miranda. Congratulations!!! I am so proud of you, well done!!

With lots of Love,

Dr. Josephine Kyambadde.

Introduction

Why I wrote this book?

Jeremiah 1:5 "Before I formed thee in the belly I knew thee, and before thou camest forth out of the womb I sanctified thee, and I ordained thee a prophet unto the nations" (KJV)

I believe we were created for a reason, I believe we are here for a purpose for which God intended. Not necessarily to be prophets like the verse above says but to be something. God created you for a mission/purpose which you have to discover and then fulfill.

I wrote this book to encourage people particularly those who have never taken time out to reflect why they were created. Those who believe that there is a reason to their existence but do not know it and those who have asked numerous questions wondering what life is all about.

The information provided in this book is to encourage you to understand that there is a purpose to your life and to find out what that purpose is. When you find your purpose, it gives you a greater reason to live.

For a long time, I was actually not sure why I was here on earth and did not know what my purpose was. I had never thought about it. I had never reflected on life and its meaning until one day one of my mentors asked me these questions; What is the purpose of your life, What is the reason as to why you exist, Why are you on this planet for? I had no answer to those questions. I went blank . . . This was a challenge that took me to a journey of introspection and with the guidance of the Holy Spirit I eventually understood the reason why I am here.

Most of People's lives are full of activities that distract them from discovering the primary reason why they are here. People study and get degrees, marry, have kids, run a business, become actors, musicians and doctors without having an understanding of whether or not those are the primary reasons as to why they exist. Writing this book is to encourage the readers who have not discovered their purpose yet to find out why they exist and what is it that they were created to do on this planet.

CHAPTER 1

The Long Road Home

"The purpose of our lives is to be happy."

Dalai Lama

Men and women have been fighting, striving, and ultimately searching for meaning within their lives. The traditional answers to the most common questions that these same people have asked since the dawn of time, such as, 'Why are we here?' have ranged far and wide.

- 'Because you exist.'
- 'I think, therefore I am.'
- 'Because God loves you.'
- 'To do good.'
- And the list goes on and on.

For every individual who has ever lived and asked that particular question, there have been untold answers, all ranging from God's purpose to random chaos.

The first question that anyone should consider answering is where your beliefs lie at the moment.

Do you believe in God?

Do you believe in random chaos?

Do you believe in a combination of the two?

There is something inherently fragile in life, at least to the point of life itself. The spirit, spirituality, and even the Purpose in life are completely separate entities to the actual physical life.

Ultimately, when talking about the fragility of life, it refers to the heart, the blood, the bones, and the elements that make up a person, an animal, or other creature.

These things are fragile. These things can lose their battle in a blink of an eye, with the simple misdirection, misstep, or mistake.

Life is surrounded by false steps just waiting to be taken. If you were to think about the last ten years of your own life, could you name five or ten or even twenty missteps that could have gone the other way and cost you everything?

So why are we here?

Why are you here?

The journey out

> *"When I chased after money, I never had enough. When I got my life on purpose and focused on giving of myself and everything that arrived into my life, then I was prosperous."*
>
> **Wayne Dyer**

When we are children, when we are young and learning about all of the things that make up our life, when we are seeking to understand the rules and the composition and the eternity of all things, we are sheltered.

We are protected. At least to some degree.

We are told and taught about a great many things, from math to science, our language, rules and regulations, authority, and so much more. We are taught these things for more than one purpose.

The first it to help ensure that one of those missteps that lay waiting for us in the world don't swallow us whole when it comes time for us to take that step towards the edge.

The other is to prepare us for our own journey out into the great open world, not just beyond our physical doors of the home we live in, but also of our spiritual world, the one where meaning, and Purpose reside.

If you look back on your childhood, do you recall what it was that you wanted to be?

Many of us had aspirations to have a great Purpose in life, to be heroes, stars, saviours of the world, or at least of the people who are important in our lives.

Some of the most common things that children aim to be when they grow up include:

- Firefighters,
- Police Officers,
- Rock Stars,
- Movie Stars,
- Astronauts,
- Award-winning Scientists,
- And so much more.

These things hold passion for us. They hold some dream of doing great deeds for the world, for ourselves, or for others. As children, we look to these professions as the true meaning of life, the Purpose that we should all hope to pursue.

Yet as we grow up, as we learn more about the world around us, and the reality that life throws within our path, we lose sight of these simple treasures that we once held close to our hearts.

We end up being something else, something different.

It doesn't mean that we end up being less than we imagine as children . . . it only means that it is different.

Life throws obstacles in our path and we are forced to make adjustments, not only in our life, but also within our minds and hearts. Most of us end up becoming:

- Teachers,
- Accountants,
- Politicians,
- Plumbers,
- Construction workers,
- Post Office employees,
- Nursing Assistants (carers)
- Security guards
- And more.

Sacrifices are made. At first, they are minor sacrifices, the kind that are small at first. Then, over time, they become bigger, more significant.

It's those little moments in life that we have to make choices, usually out of necessity, but then out of desire. These desires could be for adoration, money, status, material possessions, or any number of things, but they exist just the same.

It's when we journey out into the world that we begin to lose ourselves, we lose our focus and often—far too often—we lose our Purpose in life.

There is an alternative, of course, which is to avoid the temptations and the rigors of working day in and day out trying to make ends meet, trying to acquire the things that make us happy, but what will that get us and where?

No, life is a journey and it's a destination. If we fail to step out into the world, into the temptations and dangers and all those potential missteps that exist along the way, then we will never find out our Purpose in life. We will never become what we were intended to become, either by our own desires and designs or by those of something else, something more powerful than us, and more powerful than we can imagine that is in line with our beliefs.

When we take those important steps out into the great wide open world, we are opening ourselves up to possibilities, to hope, to dreams, and to the inevitable question that will one day face us at the moment of our greatest weakness.

Why are we here?

What is our Purpose here?

By venturing out into the world, we are able to explore this possibility with wonder, breadth, and awe. We are able to challenge ourselves and our faith and beliefs. We are able to see what possibilities exist beyond the world that we knew as children; that limited existence that hides so much from our view.

We must journey out in order to come home.

No blinders

> *"I went to a bookstore and asked the saleswoman, "Where's the self-help section?" She said if she told me, it would defeat the purpose."*
>
> **George Carlin**

Yet our journey out into the world means that we can get lost.

Whenever you step into the world, you step into the possibility that you will get lost, and that's not necessarily a bad thing, getting lost.

Getting lost means that we can find ourselves. Somewhere in all of the questions lies the route back home, back-not to where we came from-but to where we belong.

When we are lost in the world, we can find our true Purpose.

Why?

Think about it this way:

When you're traveling down a road in an unfamiliar part of the world, maybe it's a town that you've never been to before, and you take several side roads to try a change in scenery.

Like your own life as an adult, free of the rules and confines of being under parental guidance and structure; and while everything looks great and you are seeing the world that you may not have seen any other way, you are lost.

You take a few more turns, assuming that at some point you will end up on a road that leads to signs that bring you back to civilization, back to the places that you know best. But that doesn't happen.

You keep turning. You keep twisting and you're getting deeper and deeper into unknown territory. At first, you were studying houses or the trees or the mountains and lakes that surrounded you, that you passed by.

But now you are only hoping to get back to where you started so that you can get on with the rest of your trip. A part of you right now regrets having taken those side roads because you begin to wonder if you'll ever get back on track, if you'll ever get back to the life that you knew and were comfortable with.

So, finally, as dusk begins to settle in around you and you're thoroughly behind schedule and maybe somewhat frightened, you spot a small diner, or gas station, or convenience store, and you pull in for directions.

You get your directions, you write them down, and you are on your way. Within ten or fifteen minutes, you're back to the road that you know and you can breathe a sigh of relief.

When you finally reach your destination, you can sit back and relive the journey that you just made. You can recall the reflection of the mountain as smooth as a glass pond. You can recall the people working the land, tilling the soil by hand, and the family that worked and laughed together as you drove by.

You can recall every turn and every new place that you discovered and think about your own life, where you live, and what you do with your time on this Earth.

You can think about your own Purpose.

Getting lost in life helps us to take the blinders off that we put on when we are young. As children, we tend to take on the roles that our parents or our guardians place upon us.

These blinders are intended to keep us safe, but they can go a long way towards helping us get lost.

Let's rewind for a moment to that example of driving and getting lost. Let's say that, instead of deliberately taking the wrong turn, you had an address that you were trying to find, but forget it.

You think you remember it, but when you get to a fork in the road, you aren't sure. The blinders are on and you take a turn.

Unknown to you, it's the wrong turn. But that's okay because you ultimately found it, but in the process you took those blinders off and saw a world that you otherwise would not have seen.

Isn't that a wonderful concept? A wonderful notion? To strip away the blinders, the preconceived notions about things surrounding our life and in the process discovering possibilities that we never would have otherwise known existed.

Sometimes, in order to find ourselves, we have to get lost. Then we can find our way home.

The Long Road Home

Home shouldn't be thought of as a place. An address.

Home is a state of mind. It exists with the purpose of our life. Home is the place in which we surround ourselves, insulate ourselves, and protect ourselves from the unknown.

When was the last time you ventured out into an unknown existence, whether it was changing careers, relocating to a new place or country, finding a new business with which to purchase items or things that you needed or wanted, or went on a date (when you were single)?

When you did venture out, did you make plans beforehand? Did you have an escape route? A map? Safety measures?

Sometimes when you do these things, when you create a net of protection around yourself or around those things that are unknown to you, you inevitably shelter your life, even when stepping out into that great unknown.

Your Purpose doesn't necessarily exist in the unknown, but often it requires shaking off the safety gear to dig to its core.

Your Purpose is within you already, but it has been covered and clouded by an enormous quantity of thoughts, ideas, desires, directions, beliefs and so many more things that you have experienced naturally through the normal course of your life that it has become clouded over.

Finding 'home' again is a journey that cannot begin until you take the first tender and oftentimes small steps away from your home.

Finding 'home' requires you to venture out into that great unknown, into the very life that causes you fear, consternation, or trepidation.

Finding 'home' demands that you take a *leap of faith*.

And there you have it, at its most basic.

Faith

When you step out through the front doors of your home, of your shelter, of your security and comfort, when you ask the most basic and most important questions within your life, you are relying on faith.

This doesn't mean religious faith. It can, of course, but it doesn't require it.

Your Purpose exists within you, but in order to find it, you have to leave what's comfortable for a while. When you do, and when you return home, you will find that your Purpose will be there in plain sight.

It may be exactly what you've been doing all along. It may be something completely different. It may have nothing to do with your current career, family, or educational life. It may have everything to do with those things.

You may have more money, material possessions than you could know what to do with, but if you don't have your Purpose, you will feel empty.

If you have your Purpose, you will never struggle to make ends meet. When you have your Purpose, you will find the true definition of being happy.

So let's take this journey. Let's step away from your 'home.' Let's step into the world of possibilities.

Your Turn

Think back on your youth for a moment. Can you recall some of the things that you always wanted to do with your life? Those things could have been pipe dreams or simple fantasies that you never really believe would happen in the first place. On the other hand, hidden within them there could be truth that you seek.

List as many things as you can recall of what you wanted to be or do when you were growing up.

_____

_____

_____

_____

_____

_____

_____

_____

_____

CHAPTER 2

What's Your Purpose?

*"Efforts and courage are not enough without purpose
and direction."*

John F. Kennedy

If you're reading this book, it is more likely to mean that you are searching for purpose. You are striving to find and uncover meaning within and to your life.

It doesn't mean that your life, to this point, has been without some kind of purpose, however. In fact, most people will soon realize that every life, no matter what the person has done with their time in life so far, has had some kind of purpose.

But there is a marked difference between having some purpose and knowing your own Purpose in life.

The capitalization of the word Purpose throughout this book is (pardon the pun) on purpose. It is to highlight the fact that there are many different levels of purpose that a person has and goes through with his or her life, but there is only one ultimate Purpose.

You could grow up, go to college, become a nurse, find a wonderful husband, or a wife, get married, have children, raise those children to be well-adjusted, strong and independent adults who then go out in search of their own meaning in life.

Their own Purpose.

Those are purposes that you had in life. They were important to you, you cherished them, and focused on giving those things and people the best opportunities for success.

But they may not have been your ultimate Purpose in life.

Ask yourself the following questions:

- Are you content? Do you wake up every morning feeling as though that, no matter what you do that day, you are going to be happy?
- Do you wake up in the middle of the night feeling that something is missing from your life?

- Are you restless? Do you wish to get out from your current town? To move away and start over?

- Do you sometimes fantasize about a different job? A career change?

- Are you spending more time thinking about how others have it 'so good' and you're just scraping by?

- Do you find yourself envying your neighbours or friends for the possessions and things that they have?

- Are you bored with yourself? Your family? Your life?

- Do you try new things all the time, hoping to find something that interests you?

- Are you restless?

If any of these questions rings true for you, then you are seeking Purpose in your life. Something has been missing, but that doesn't mean that your life has been empty. It only means that you haven't yet found what you were put on this Earth to do.

That's right. You were put on this Earth for a Purpose.

A question of Belief?

> "As far as we can discern, the sole purpose of human existence
> is to kindle a light in the darkness of mere being."
>
> **Carl Jung**

There are literally hundreds of different religions around the world. There have been thousands that have existed throughout history and most of them have all been based on the same philosophy: finding Purpose.

When a man and a woman first found themselves wandering the great wide-open expanse of the world, it was a frightening place to be.

There were untold unknowns throughout the world and places that few even had the courage to explore.

The night sky swallowed sight and offered brilliance within the stars that shined down in return. The moon and the sun would rise in the east and set in the west. Sometimes they would chase each other. Other times it seemed as though the sun had won and the moon was in hiding.

The oceans rolled in and then exhaled out. Teeming within the depths of the water would be creatures that would swallow men whole and legends would be born.

Animals that provided sustenance in the form of meat could also bring the end of life for the unwitting or unlucky. As men and women developed language and culture, they also began to know other emotions than fear.

They began to know hope and envy. Lust and jealousy. They began to look to themselves and to those around them and try to measure what they had compared to what others had.

And ultimately they would all look at death with anxiety, fear, and wonder.

What happens in the next life? Is there a next life? What does this all mean? What do we leave behind as our legacy?

Which all leads to the ultimate question that we are still seeking to answer to this day.

What is our Purpose?

Some believe God created all life and that He also gave each one of us a Purpose within our own life. Still others believe that there is no Purpose to life but the one we make for ourselves.

What do you believe?

If you are searching for the answers to these questions, if you are searching for *your* Purpose in life, then you have already answered that question.

You believe that you were put on this Earth for a specific reason. That explains the restlessness that you feel. That explains the envy that you may experience within your heart; the one that leaves you measuring yourself against others, trying to gain an advantage or somehow come out on top.

There is a purpose within your life. There are many, actually, but we all have One Purpose and there is no single person that can tell us what it is.

You don't have to believe in God to find your Purpose. While God may have given you that single Purpose, it doesn't require your faith to exist.

It already does exist.

But you are not going to find the answer to your Purpose between the pages of any book. You won't find your Purpose by talking to ministers, pastors, or priests.

You won't find your purpose enrolling in college as an aging adult.

You won't find it through discussion groups.

You won't find your Purpose through therapy sessions with your local psychiatrists, or counsellors.

You won't find your Purpose by watching television and hoping that it just 'comes to you.'

Your Purpose can only be found when you stop, take a moment to explore the world around you, from everyday happenings to the physical, from the thoughts and aspirations that you once had as a child to the dreams that soon encompassed your life as an adult, from the sacrifices you made and somehow understanding what they were and what they have to do with your current situation.

Will those with faith in God find their Purpose easier than those without?

That's an important question to ask, so let's explore.

Finding answers

> "I do not have much patience with a thing of beauty that must be explained to be understood. If it does need additional interpretation by someone other than the creator, then I question whether it has fulfilled its purpose."
>
> **Charlie Chaplin**

Who is God?

To some, God is an entity, a super natural being who can read thoughts, who designed the universe, and placed us all here for a specific Purpose in life.

To others, God is an idea, the concept of something that we cannot explain nor truly understand. God is a host of ideas and a rich discovery of meaning hidden somewhere within the tapestry of existence.

To others God is a Super Natural Being who cannot be defined or described.

To some, God exists so that men and women wouldn't have to feel too alone within their own life. To these people, God is a fiction and Purpose is precisely what you make it.

Let me ask another question for a moment. If God doesn't exist and He doesn't have a greater Purpose for your own existence, then why would anyone feel the need to discover their own Purpose in life?

Put another way, if there was no God, then there would be no Purpose. Correct?

After all, if we are only here out of a random set of circumstances that collided together to form our essence, then whatever we *wanted* to do with our lives should be enough to give us Purpose . . . Huh?

This idea makes perfect sense to some people, right? Of course it does. If we wanted to have the nice, four-bedroom house high on the hilltop, with the view of the ocean in the distance, a gentle stream rolling by, and children laughing and playing throughout it, then that would be our Purpose. Or it could be, correct?

We could decide on our own what our Purpose is.

We wouldn't need to discover it because it would only exist by our own design.

So, for those that don't believe in God, or the existence of some greater spiritual power that guides our lives, then why are you reading a book on finding Purpose?

You already have your Purpose. It's whatever you want it to be.

If you still don't feel that you've found it and that there *is* a specific reason why you are here, then you believe in something beyond yourself that guides you, encourages you, and has some measure of design for your life.

Don't look now, but you have *faith*.

Answers are found rooted in the essence of faith.

Scientists who explore the universe looking for answers as to why we are here, why we exist, and how we came to be, all have faith.

This doesn't mean that they have faith in God, or gods, or some existential being that formed everything with His Will. No, faith isn't a word that is bound to religion or spirituality. Faith can be applied to so many other factors beyond the obvious.

But these scientists must have faith in order to explore the universe, our history, and the unknown world around us.

Their faith comes out through theory.

Have you heard of the Big Bang Theory? This is the idea that the universe was born out of one massive explosion of gasses that collapsed upon each other and forged all planets and stars and matter that exists today.

It's a theory that hasn't been proven. Just as the theory of evolution. It hasn't been proven.

They all rely on faith. And though none of these theories have been proven, none of them have been proven false, either. Which brings us inexorably back to faith.

Faith is about accepting possibilities without concrete answers. Faith is about believing in something when the questions haven't even been answered. Faith is about discovering something within ourselves while exploring something beyond ourselves, and greater than ourselves at the same time.

Who is God? What is spirituality? What happens to us after we die? What is our Purpose in life?

These are questions that no one can answer *for* you. People can certainly share their beliefs with you. People can share their own ideas with you, but no one can *tell* you what to believe, or what to ignore.

Those are things that you have to do for yourself.

Sometimes we find that the answers were sitting within us all along, waiting for release but were not going to show themselves until we took a leap of faith.

Believing that you have a Purpose in life and that you were put here for some specific reason, is faith.

It is faith at its core.

It is the essence that you must accept if you are to have any hope of finding your true Purpose in life.

No one can tell you what your Purpose is. You have to find that answer on your own.

You have to discover it in your own time, in your own place, within your own heart. Your Purpose won't be the same as someone else's Purpose, even if you want it to be.

Maybe your best friend's Purpose was to help children by becoming a teacher, and maybe you love the idea of teaching, and pursued a degree in education, secured a job on a school, and are an exceptional teacher, but you still feel as though you haven't found your Purpose.

This doesn't mean that your life is meaningless; it only means that you were trying to find your Purpose with your *head*, not your *heart*.

Your heart is where faith lies. Your heart is where the answer to this question of Purpose resides.

It is your heart that you have to explore and to listen to, and in life, we become so consumed by living that we forget how to listen to our heart.

And that is the answer to the first question of finding your Purpose.

Listen to your *heart* and you will find your Purpose.

So how do we strip away all the noise and clutter that congests our inner ear? That causes our heart to be overpowered?

We take steps. We walk outside the door of our life. We explore the world around us. In time, all the things that we thought were important slip away and we find what was written on our hearts from the dawn of time. We find the imprint left behind by what made us.

That is how we find our Purpose. If you're ready to take this journey, then you're not alone. Let's take that first step together.

Your Turn

There are things that you *want* to do with your life, and then there are things that you *must* do with your life. Family obligations, paying the rent, and all of the other necessities that exist can cloud our Purpose.

What are some of the things that you feel trap you where you are in your life? List them here (and when we mention 'trap', it isn't a negative thing, such as being a parent to young children 'trap' you in a certain role).

_____

_____

_____

_____

_____

_____

_____

_____

CHAPTER 3

What's the Truth About Money?

*"All successful people men and women are big dreamers.
They imagine what their future could be, ideal in every
respect, and then they work every day toward their
distant vision, that goal or purpose."*

Brian Tracy

Have you ever thought about money? Of course you have; it's one of the necessities of modern life in order to survive. We all need money. That's the fact that not a single one of us can escape. But that doesn't answer the underlying question of whether you have honestly thought about money.

Do you know what the purpose of money is? Do you know where it came about, why it was created, and how the idea of money has changed over the course of history? If you haven't taken the time to understand this basic premise of the most important currency for millions of people around the world, then it's time that you did. Understanding the truth about money can help you clear the landscape around your own life and the reasons that make it difficult to find Purpose within our own realities.

How many times in your life have you heard people tell you, tell themselves, or tell others that you have to have money in order to be happy? Coupled along with that is the ever-popular statement that 'Money is the root of all evil.'

Yet evil has existed since the dawn of time, yet money has not existed nearly as long, so it would be safe to say that money is, in fact, *not* the root of all evil. Money can corrupt, however. It can cloud vision, ideas, morals, and values and in most societies, people spend most of their energy in search of money and more money and that is one of the easiest ways to lose sight of your Purpose.

Money, at its core, is nothing more than a symbol. Money represents value that someone possesses. In certain parts of the world, money isn't a factor, as they trade, barter, and exchange other products or services, as had been done for millennia throughout most of the world.

Throughout the greater part of the history of mankind, people subsisted not in trading coins or other forms of money, but in trading goods and services.

If you were a shepherd, then you traded wool sheared from your sheep or you traded your sheep for things that you needed.

If your neighbour was a farmer and grew tomatoes, wheat, and other food items that were essential to your survival, then you were likely to have traded for those things with the wool or the sheep that you raised. In those days, you needed to possess something that others wanted in order to survive effectively within a community. If you didn't have anything that the farmer wanted or needed, then you may have traded your physical services, or those of your children to work the soil on the farm in exchange for food to put on the table.

If that wasn't ideal for the farmer still, then you were more likely to go out into your community in search of the things that the farmer wanted or needed and would begin to barter and make deals to acquire those items or services that would earn you food to feed your family.

Before money, life was spent trying to find a niche that filled the necessities of your existence, such as food, shelter, water, and other life essentials.

Then money came along and changed the entire course of history. When the shepherd could *sell* his wool or sheep to merchants in the center of town, then he would take that money and go to the farmer and purchase the food he wanted, even if the farmer needed nothing from the shepherd personally or directly.

Money made the act of work much easier for most people and it allowed them to buy items that they wanted, even if they didn't *need* them from other merchants who would otherwise not have much interest in wool or sheep, for example.

Over time, money became the normal currency of trade throughout many regions of the world. It also began its steady march towards corruption of certain individuals.

When people learned that they could buy items that they wanted with money, and that there were realistically no limits on the type of items that they could purchase with money, then they began to covet the things that they didn't have, but perhaps their neighbours had, or leaders within their community had.

When people began to have money, they wanted more money and they either worked harder, charged more, or used other means to gather as much money as they could possibly get their hands on to buy all of the things that they wanted. They didn't care about whether they needed it. If they wanted something and it cost a certain amount of money, then its value was determined by that factor.

Think about this in terms of modern society. We, as a society, are surrounded by advertisements promising new and improved, this item is better than that item, or savings that we won't even believe. Everything that we need in life has a price tag on it. Yet not everything that has a monetary value is accurate, at least not in the sense of needs and wants.

Supply and demand

> *"Be above it! Make the world serve your purpose, but do not serve it."*
>
> **Johann Wolfgang von Goethe**

When you turn on the television or walk down the aisle of a shopping centre, you are inundated with advertisements for dozens of items. Some will seem so cheap that you can't pass up the deal while others cause you to shake your head in amazement, disbelieving that anyone would pay the asking price for an item so unattractive or unnecessary.

Yet most of the value for items that exist today are driven by supply and demand. When oil prices around the world rose to extraordinary levels, it was about supply and demand. The oil producing nations in the Middle-East had determined that they would cut the production of their oil supply because they felt that the price was too low.

The price per barrel of oil skyrocketed but then people around the world began to use less oil by driving less, heating their homes less, and other means to cut back and this brought the price back down.

The oil was still the same, but the demand had changed and that change in demand dictated the price.

When you desire something, some material item, and more and more people also desire the same item, then the price will invariably rise to meet the demand being placed on that item. This doesn't mean that the product or service is better than it was when it was cheaper, it only means that more people want the item now.

When more people begin to *desire* something, then the price of that product increases. When that happens, the inherent *value* of the money that you hold in your hand goes down.

Think about it this way: when you were able to purchase gasoline/petrol for your vehicle at 70Pence per gallon/litre, your pounds bought you more fuel for your car. When the price went up to £1.30 per litre, your money could only buy you one-quarter of the fuel that it could when the price was 70Pence. The fuel is the same; it's the money that has changed.

In modern society, there are a number of things that we need in order to live comfortably. Notice how the word 'survive' was left out of that statement. In life, there are few things that you realistically need in order to survive.

You need air, water, food. Beyond that, everything else is considered non-necessities.

But what about clothing and shelter? What about a car to get to work? What about electricity and heat or television?

These are common questions that people would have who have grown up in a society that values these things as necessities even though they are merely luxuries. The only things that you need in order to survive are air to breathe, water for your body, and food for nutrition for your body.

You don't need clothing in order to stay alive.

You don't need housing or shelter in the form of the large Mansion, the five bedroom house with four-and-a-half baths for you and your spouse, you don't need two fifty thousand pound sports car to get to your job. Those things are not necessities.

If you were to take off from home on a nice warm summer day, hike into the remote part of the world, strip down all your clothing and leave everything behind, but new what fruits to eat, how to find water, and how to hunt for other food necessities, then you would live for a long time.

You wouldn't die because there was no television. You wouldn't die because there were no books. You wouldn't die because you didn't have your D&G sunglasses or shoes or fine mink coats. You would live and you might actually live better than you were when you were merely chasing the materialistic aspects that modern society has deemed important and necessary.

Money has clouded the idea of what is important in our lives because we, as a society, have become detached from the actual processes of survival.

When you're hungry, you head down to the store to buy food or you wander into any number of fast food restaurants and grab a combo meal. You don't have to worry about where it came from, who is growing what, or determining whether you have something that they might want in exchange for your next meal.

There are millions of people throughout the world who don't know where their next meal will come from. They may go days and days without eating, hoping that they will be able to find food before too long, but they don't know how to get it because there are droughts or wars or famines that have crippled their communities' ability to grow food.

With money, you look at the price and when more people want the same item, it will be more expensive and your pound will be worth less. If fewer people want the item, then it will be cheaper and your pound will be worth more.

This is the essence of supply and demand. Yet the truth about money and faith and your Purpose are somewhat different and it's important to explore this differential.

Money, Faith, and Purpose

> *"I love to shop after a bad relationship.*
> *I don't know. I buy a new outfit and it*
> *makes me feel better. It just does.*
> *Sometimes I see a really great outfit, I'll*
> *break up with someone on purpose."*
>
> **Rita Rudner**

In our modern culture, it has become far too easy to become lost in the midst of money. As mentioned already, people think of things as being necessities in life that aren't at all necessary.

Cultures have deemed clothing to be necessity, but not because we would die if we didn't wear any, but because of humility. Puritans were aghast at the idea of a person walking about in public showing their skin. To them, the only skin that should be shown would be the face and hands. Everything else was meant to be shared only between a husband and wife.

Other cultures find that clothing our bodies is necessary, but that also nudity is entirely acceptable to some.

Yet fashion designers spend enormous amounts of money to create new fashions, new designs, colours, styles and so much more every year and what they are doing is preying upon the weak individuals who feel that they must buy these items in order to be attractive.

Society has pressed upon them that their value or status within that society is measured in the type of clothing, the designers that they wear, just as those same people believe that the type of car they drive will grant them a higher place in society, or within their community or social network of friends.

If you have ever purchased a car because of how you thought others would perceive you when you're behind the wheel, and you didn't really enjoy the car, then you were a victim of this superficiality.

Money has distorted the sense of need and want to the point where everyone seems to be competing with others to have the nice clothing, the fancy car, the big house, and all of those material possessions. The problem with this is that the reason for all of this empty desire is to fill a void inside that will never be filled, no matter how much money you have.

Because all of those items that you purchase are merely symbols of money that you have, or had. They are symbols of wealth.

When you are pursuing a status symbol or a status within your community or inner circle of friends, you are allowing money to be your main purpose in existence. You are allowing money to determine what you do and how you do it.

People choose careers based on the amount of money that they could make throughout their lives. Some of the highest paying career jobs are:

- Doctors
- Lawyers
- Engineers
- Politicians
- Celebrities

If you asked people whom you pass on the street what they think about these types of people, you'll likely be met with positive attributes.

- Intelligent
- Wealthy
- Classy
- Important
- Successful

These are just a few of the terms that you are likely to hear associated with these professions. Wealthy is one of the most prominent, because people measure success on a person's wealth.

Not many people consider a carpenter as being someone important because he or she wouldn't make a great deal of money. Yet Jesus was a carpenter and He is one of the most important people in the history of the world.

Money has the ability to distort and cloud Purpose. If you are focused on making as much money as you can in your life, then you will have a difficult time finding your Purpose.

In the Bible, God considers money to be an idol that people worship and that they shouldn't worship idols. There's a reason for this. When you worship idols, then you are not worshipping God.

When you place money above all other things in your life, then you are giving in to the temptation that swallows lives and ruins souls. The stories are all around us about people who thought they would be happy with their money, and worked hard to earn it, but learned that it didn't bring them happiness. They learned that it only brought them more sorrow and heartache.

They had allowed money to be more important than finding their Purpose in life. If you want to find your Purpose in life, then you need to let go of the idea that money is the most important thing to attain.

You need food, but you don't need to eat in the fanciest restaurants. You need water, but you don't need to buy £3 bottled water. You need air, but you don't need specially filtered air just because you have heard that it is healthier for your skin.

Shelter is a good thing, but you don't need the mansion at the top of the hill that forces you to spend every penny that you earn on the mortgage.

A car is important if your job is several miles from your home, but you don't need the sports car or the Hummer to get there.

When you strip away all the excess and realize and accept that money is nothing more than a symbol, a deceptive idol that people worship as they seek to fill the void inside, then you will be able to find your Purpose, and find faith that you may feel is missing from your life.

Your Turn

What are some of the things that you have measured your worth against others with? It could be a car, makeup, clothing. It could be your spouse. Some people marry not for true love or that deep emotional connection, but because the person is extraordinarily attractive or wealthy. List the things that you have pursued, purchased, or desired because of what they would make others think of you. How did you benefit from those things? Did they fill up the void in you?

_____

_____

_____

_____

_____

_____

_____

_____

_____

CHAPTER 4

Passion and Principles

"I am here for a purpose and that purpose is to grow into a mountain, not to shrink to a grain of sand. Henceforth will I apply ALL my efforts to become the highest mountain of all and I will strain my potential until it cries for mercy."

Og Mandino

What are your principles? What are the basic core beliefs that define you?

When asked this question, many people gaze back and remain silent. The reason for this is simple: they don't have an answer.

That's completely alright at this point in time, too. You don't need to have an answer to that question, just as you don't need to have an answer to what you Purpose is in life right now.

The question about principles is often met with silence because in our cultural society, as discussed in the previous chapter, has been clouded by the ultimate pursuit of money, or status. Money and status go hand-in-hand today. If you don't have money, you don't generally have much social status. If you do have money, your status is elevated regardless of what you do.

Can you measure a person's principles through his or her actions? It happens everyday where we see a person who is entrusted with power or control over others and takes advantage of their position.

This person may steal money from a fund, they may lie about their affairs, or they might even cheat on their spouse, all while telling the world a different story.

So when we see someone like this on the television or in the paper, can we measure their principles by their actions or their words?

The answer is simple: by their actions. There's a phrase that goes along with this notion and it is: "Actions speak louder than words."

So, let's ask this question once again. What are your principles?

Are you the type of person who works countless hours in the day on your job? Do you prefer to spend time at your office than spend it with family?

Do you covet the money that you earn with these extra hours? If so, then your principles might be to put work before family.

Are you the type of person who would rather lay around on the couch and watch daytime television rather than put in an honest day's work to earn money? Would you rather let the government, or other people such as family members, pay for the things you need than earn it yourself? If so, then your principles might be laziness first.

Are you the type of person who enjoys judging other people based on their appearance, job, or race? Do you find yourself making nasty comments to friends about someone else? Then you may be insecure with yourself or you may believe that you're better than other people. Your principles may be about keeping yourself elevated above those other people.

Principles define what we do in life. If you don't think that you have any principles, or they are just background noise, then you are doing yourself a great disservice. Principles are the core of what any of us do. We cannot get away from our principles, no matter what we do in life.

If you are the type of person who would cheat on a test rather than study, but decry those who cheat on their taxes, then your principles are confused.

If you go around preaching a simple life to others, but go home to your Waterford crystal or your five thousand pound entertainment system, then your principles are confused.

How you find your Purpose in life relies heavily on the principles that you have adopted, or consciously adopt. There's no reason that anyone who wanted to could change their core principles. In fact, if your principles are not in line with whom you wish to be, then it's important to change them so that they are in line with whom you want to be.

Whom you want to be, and who you are, will often fight each other whether you realize it or not and this will often block you from finding your purpose.

Principles without passion lead to an empty and hollow life. You don't want that. You don't want that emptiness, that void within your life, that's why you have taken up the pursuit of finding your Purpose. You know that something has been missing and you want to know what it is that is missing.

You can have great principles, too, but you may only have taken on those principles because they made sense at the time, or because you want to be a good person, though you may not believe in them.

That is principles without passion. It will help you move through life, but it won't help you find your Purpose.

What are principles?

"If you're alive, there's a purpose for your life."

Rick Warren

People often confuse principles with desires. Some people want to get ahead in life, in their jobs, win over the gorgeous woman, get the nice apartment on the top floor of the high rise, or any other type of measurement for life success, but these aren't principles.

Those are desires.

Principles are *ideals* that are absolute. They can't be altered or adjusted to meet a change in the person's life or lifestyle. If those changes occur, then they are no longer the same principles.

Do no harm is a principle.

Do unto others as you'd have done unto yourself is a principle.

I will not steal is a principle.

I will not cheat is a principle.

Each person can have one guiding principle or several, but they are to be considered absolutes.

If you have the principle that you will not cheat, and then turn around and fudge a few numbers on your tax return so that it saves you some money, then you don't really have that principle in your life.

If you have a principle that you will do no harm, but constantly weave in and out of traffic, speeding on your way to work or on your way home or wherever you're going, then you're doing harm to someone. You are putting someone else at risk with the choice that you make.

When you break your own principles, then they are no longer your principles.

They may be guidelines that you would like to live by, but they are not principles.

Not every principle is easy to live by, now should they be easy to live by? Principles, just by their very nature of being absolute, are difficult. They challenge us to be better people, better friends, better lovers, better citizens. Principles are the foundation upon which we build our lives and even if you don't think you have any real, strong principles at this point in your life, you're wrong.

Everyone has principles. Some have the principle that they will do or say anything they have to in order to get ahead in their job. Some have the principle that they will act in whatever way is necessary in order to be liked, or to be popular. Some people will have the principle that it's okay to cheat a little, as long as it doesn't go too far, or they don't get caught.

Those are all principles that people do have, even though they will rarely ever openly admit that they are their guiding principles.

Look to the politicians throughout the world who have been caught committing some kind of crime against the people, whether it's embezzlement, bribery, voter fraud, or more. These people all have the same defense, that they are not guilty, it wasn't them, that their political opponent framed them. When the evidence is presented and it's clear that they are guilty, they then fall back on the base that they were weak, they gave in to temptation, or they were caught up in power and opportunity. They are always sorry in the end, but they never admit that was their principle.

But the rest of the world knows better. Yes, we do. Principles are the ideals that you live by and they cant change all of the time. That's why it is so important to know what your principles are and to define them and to make a concerted effort every day that you wake up to follow those principles and see them through.

Anybody who lives in the modern world knows that it is not easy to live with positive principles every single day. There are temptations all around us, from trying to make a few easy pounds to lusting after a person who is not your husband or your wife. Life throws many challenges in our path.

There are a million roads that lead to hell, but it is our principles that will guide us away from it and towards better places in our lives, and to the world beyond this life.

If you don't have a passion for your principles, then you are going to find it extremely difficult to follow through with them.

You can't hold principles that belong to someone else unless you truly, honestly, believe in them yourself. If your parents believed that cheating was never okay, no matter what the circumstances, and yet you see your friends cheat on tests, get better grades than you, and never get caught, then you might see it differently.

You may continue to avoid cheating, even though you don't believe that it hurts anyone. In this case, you don't have passion for that principle and even though you hold up that principle, the effort to maintain it becomes greater, especially when life becomes more challenging.

For example, let's say that you are in your last year of college and you have perfect grades so far. You take a course that is a requirement, but not something you care about and it's a course that is giving you trouble. You know you're not going to get a perfect grade unless you score perfectly on your final exam. You've seen your friends cheat and help each other year in and year out without ever getting caught.

You don't want your perfect grade to disappear, so you think to yourself, 'It's only a class that I had to take. It's not something that's really going to affect me the rest of my life.' So you ask for their help to cheat. Just a little. Or you're extremely tempted.

If you don't have a passion for that principle of not cheating, then you are more likely to cave in when the pressure mounts. If you do have a passion for it, you won't care who cheated and got away with it; you just won't do it for any reason.

Passion for anything in life means that there is a greater chance for success in anything that you do. When it comes to principles, having passion means you will have more strength to follow through with them even when times are tough, the road gets rough, or you feel as though you're losing your footing or balance.

Principles and Purpose

"The secret of success is constancy to purpose."

Benjamin Disraeli

Your Purpose exists. It has always existed. Life can get in the way of finding it, hearing it, and following it as you accept other beliefs or ideals or reasons for your existence, but your Purpose is still there, waiting for you to find it.

When you have the wrong principles in place, or they are constantly in flux, then it will be difficult for you to find your Purpose in life. Principles that are geared towards getting ahead in the financial world, landing the best job, having the best house, and keeping up with the neighbours and all of the material possessions that they have are principles that are going to cloud your judgment. They are going to get in the way of you finding your Purpose.

If you want to have your Purpose and know what it is clearly, then you need to develop positive principles that are in line with your faith, that are consistent with your faith, and that don't shift because of your insecurities.

We all face insecurities at one time or another in our life. It's natural. The test is to not allow those insecurities to deter us from the principles that guide us. We always have a choice when it comes to our guiding principles and when we break them, they are changed.

They aren't altered or adjusted; they are changed and the only way to change them back is to find that passion that we once had for them, if we ever did, and then change them.

When you have principles that you are passionate about and that are in line with the guiding principles of the Father, then your life will be open to your Purpose. It will become that much easier for you to find your Purpose and to live a life with Purpose.

Think of principles as the foundation stones for your Purpose. If they are cracked, then your house will fall eventually. If they are strong, if they are positive, and you have a passion for them, then your house will remain strong with them.

It's important to always be vigilant about your principles, to check and make sure that you are holding to your principles firmly, especially in the face of temptation, for when you do, you will always have a clear view of your Purpose.

Your Turn

What are your principles? Are you aware of the principles that guide your life, or have they been in the background for all of these years? Too many people simply take their principles for granted and that can lead to slips and falls throughout one's life. If you don't know what your principles are, it's time you defined them. Then determine if they are in line with the Creator and what He deems a positive principle. List your principles here.

_____

_____

_____

_____

_____

_____

_____

_____

CHAPTER 5

Career Versus Love

*"It is not how much one makes but to what purpose
one spends."*

John Ruskin

How many times have you heard someone say that they are holding off on
marriage until they build their career? It happens more and more often these
days in our modern times. Love becomes secondary to a career.

Why is this a problem? After all, a person is being responsible when they
want to wait and start their career first. They have established that in order to
be successful in life, they need to have a good career. So what is the problem
with putting career ahead of love and marriage?

A career is based on making money. It's based on building status within the
community, one's mind, to their family and friends, and so forth. A career

is about following the almighty pound and trying to make as many of those as you can.

A career is about chasing the false idols. There is no love in a career. There is only work and making money. These things can leave a person feeling empty at the end of their life.

Yes, of course there are many people who have come and gone whose passion, whose desire was all about making money or having only a career and they went to their graves feeling content with the choices they made. These people do exist, but they are the exception to the rule.

Did they find their Purpose? Did they know that they were meant to be devoted to their careers at the expense of all other things? Maybe, but most likely they were simply too clouded by their greed and desires to see what was missing.

That is the power of money and wealth. Those things can fill the void that most of us feel at some point in our lives, but it doesn't fill it with nutrition for the soul, but rather with garbage to make the soul feel full.

It's like feeding a person candy every single day. Sure, they are getting sustenance and calories, but eventually they will become ill. A body can live without certain vitamins and minerals, sometimes for decades at a time. Some people can live into their one hundreds having smoked every day of their life and never feel the harmful affects of smoking. That doesn't mean that smoking is good for you, or that it isn't harmful. It just means that some people's bodies (and in this case, their souls) respond to different things differently than other people's.

The people who devoted their life to their careers and die with no regrets may have felt as though they were full, but in fact they were likely quite empty inside. The candy that the wealth provided for their soul wasn't enough for it.

Would that be enough for you? It takes a certain kind of character, a specific type of person, to feel full and complete by devoting their life to their career.

Then there are those who might argue that people who built a career first, and then found love, were happy, contented, fulfilled and successful. The question to ask here would be whether that is completely truthful?

When you are questioning what your Purpose is in life, when you are searching for your *raison d'etre*, then you are asking the question that millions of people before you have asked. So what would be more conducive to finding your Purpose in life: finding a career that brings you money and material possessions, or finding love that can fill your soul?

What is a career?

"My passions were all gathered together like fingers that made a fist. Drive is considered aggression today; I knew it then as purpose."

Bette Davis

If we were to define what a career is, what kind of words would you use? This is an interesting exercise in what your priorities are, how you view these topics, and what you feel is important when it comes to a career. So, what are some of the aspects that many people will use to describe or define what a career is?

How about some of the following:

- Job for life
- Stability
- Financial success
- Money
- Respect
- Honour

These are just some of the topics that come to mind when trying to define what a career is to most people.

Remember, there is a major difference between a career and a job. A job is something that people do in order to pay the bills, to put food on the table, and to be able to do some of the things that they want to do with their life.

A *career* is something that you build towards and build up throughout your life. While people can change careers in the middle of their life, it doesn't happen overnight and focusing on a career requires a lot more attention and dedication and devotion than simply opening the classified section of the newspaper to find a job.

A career is a life decision. It's not like picking which movie you want to go see down at the cinema. A career is about dedicating a specific portion of your life to it, the hours and days of the week, the overtime, the sacrifices, and knowing that you will be climbing the imaginary corporate ladder with each day that you devote to your career.

A career is built over many years and will provide the person with many of the same things that a job will, such as money to buy items, security to know that you will be able to afford a specific lifestyle, and more. A career is also likely to provide a person with knowledge that is specific to that career, which can be carried from one employer to another.

If a person works in the aerospace engineering field, and they don't like the employer they are working for now, they can apply to other companies and are likely to find work with them, assuming that they are good at what they do and can prove their value to these other companies.

Even though they change jobs, they are still in the same career. A career is basically a lifelong commitment and without having a focus on career, at least to some degree, then some people might find that their life lacks meaning. It lacks Purpose.

Does this mean that a person can't find their Purpose within their career? Absolutely not. In fact, many people pursue the career that is in line with their Purpose.

The individual who designs spacecrafts that travel to the moon might very well be put on this Earth to do that very thing. God may have decided that this person's Purpose was to help others reach the stars.

The individual who stands behind the scenes of the star politician who is rising to power may be destined for that line of work. God may have decided that this particular person was ideal for the task assigned to him or her.

There are many cases where careers are perfectly in line with Purpose, but that's not the issue of this chapter. The issue here is when career replaces love in a person's life and the harm that it can do.

Love and life

> *"There's nothing wrong in suffering, if you suffer for a purpose. Our revolution didn't abolish danger or death. It simply made danger and death worthwhile."*
>
> **H. G. Wells**

Is a life without love worth living? Is a life without love complete?

These are questions that have been asked and studied for ages and each person will come to their own conclusion, of course, so it's an important question to ask yourself. Is love really all that important to life? How about to finding your Purpose in life?

There are people who believe that love is the *most* important thing in anyone's life, that a life without love is empty and meaningless, no matter what that person does with the rest of their life. Some people believe that a life without love is hollow and when there is that hollowness, those individuals will spend most of their time running from one relationship to the next, trying to find that human connection, that love, which is missing.

Other people will dive into their careers in order to find salvation of some sort or another. These are empty promises that are like the candy to the body. They may make the person feel full for a while, but they don't offer nourishment.

God is all about love. Life should be all about love. Love is the one emotion that science has failed to explain. Sure, they say that it is caused by chemicals in the body, all surging and moving throughout the blood stream, but the connection that people feel towards others when love is involved still has no explanation.

Much like the thought processes in the brain. Science can explain it in forensic terms, but they have no clue why people can think, create new ideas from nothing, or solve complex mathematical equations that have never been done before.

Love is crucial to life. Like the air that we breathe, love brings oxygen to the soul. If you live your life without love, then you will be empty and for the people that have done this, they find that they are often angry, bitter, and don't enjoy life much at all. They also don't find their Purpose in life.

Your Purpose comes through your soul and when you deprive your soul of the oxygen that it needs, then you are also depriving it of the important energy that is required to find your Purpose.

God placed us on this Earth for a reason and at His basic core, God is all about love. When you deny love within your life, you deny God from your life as well. When you deny God, then you are also denying your Purpose in life.

It is fine to choose a career; in fact, it's important to do so, but when you do this at the expense of love, when you place love second to your career, at what point will that change? At what point will you suddenly decide that love should come before career?

Good intentions are fine, but the road to hell is often paved with good intentions. A career can lead to material things and that can lead to more material things and more desires for material things. Then, when your career is doing well, you might wake up one morning and head out in search of the love that has been missing.

At that point, are you looking for true love? Or are you looking for someone who will love you for the things that you can buy for them?

If you want to find your true Purpose in life, then you need to welcome love into your life. It doesn't have to be the love of another person, *per se*, but love is necessary and should not be disregarded.

If your love is the love you have for God, then He will enlighten you on your Purpose much more clearly. If your love is the love for your husband or your wife, then you will feel the important connection that life provides and this can lead you to the path that leads you to your Purpose.

As mentioned in previous chapters, the body needs three things to survive: air, water, and food. The soul needs one: love.

Set a career in its rightful place and you will find love lightening up your life and you will be able to see your Purpose more clearly.

Your Turn

A career can be a wonderful thing. It can make you feel whole, but that feeling, without love, doesn't last. In a few words, describe how important a career is to you and why. Then, define what love is in your life and whom, if anyone, you truly love with all of your heart and soul. You may be married, but you may not truly be in love with that person. This is for your eyes only, so be honest. If you have true love in your life, can you see your Purpose?

_____

_____

_____

_____

_____

_____

_____

_____

CHAPTER 6

Burning the Candle

"Being busy does not always mean real work. The object of all work is production or accomplishment and to either of these ends there must be forethought, system, planning, intelligence, and honest purpose, as well as perspiration. Seeming to do is not doing."

Thomas A. Edison

The expression, 'burning the candle at both ends' has been around for many, many years. It basically means that a person who is burning the candle at both ends is wearing themselves out.

A candle serves a simple purpose: to provide light. When the candle is lit at both ends, it may produce a bit more light, but it's burning itself out twice as fast.

For people, when they are burning the candle at both ends, then they are doing too much, wearing themselves down, and will run out of energy, motivation, desire, or strength too soon. This doesn't serve your Purpose for being here any good. It also doesn't serve God, either, no matter what you're doing.

Every life is a candle in the world. It burns for a period of time then it is either extinguished too soon, or it runs out and the flame runs out of fuel. Your candle has been burning for many years already. Some years it has burned lightly while other years it has burned quite intensely.

Wherever you are in your life right now, take a moment to look around your life and determine whether you're burning your own candle at both ends, or if you are simply not burning it hot enough.

If you are burning your candle at both ends, it means that you are doing too much, trying to be everything to everyone at once. You are not taking the time to be objective, to allow others to help you. Some people will argue that there is no one else to help them out, so they have no choice but to burn their candle at both ends.

Which leads to the question on why? Why do you feel that it's necessary to burn the candle at both ends? Is it to keep up with your work? With your career? Is it to get your children from school to music lessons, back to school for their sports practice, then to get them home, make sure that they are doing their homework while you make sure that they have something to eat that night, then finally, once you get them to bed you can actually start doing the work that you need to be doing yourself?

While these actions are commendable, most of them are not necessary. Most of them are only designed to help keep some reputation that you hold for yourself. Are the children reliant solely on you to get them to their lessons or practice? Is there no one else who could help out?

Often, there are many people within our circle who would be more than willing to help out if we asked. That would mean that you would have to ask and yet, for some reason, it seems to be too much for some people to do . . . to ask for help.

Why? What is the hang up that people have about asking others for assistance? It is this hang up, this difficulty that people have, which causes them to struggle too much, to work too hard, and end up burning the candle at both ends.

If you are not burning the candle hot enough, you are being lazy and waiting for life to come to you. You may be unmotivated by certain things in your life, or you may be somewhat lost, looking for your Purpose.

The problem with not burning your candle hot enough is that a dim candle doesn't produce much light. How are you ever going to find your Purpose in life if you are not working towards anything?

It's easy to sit on the sidelines and watch life and point to one person or another and say to ourselves, 'That's what I want to do' or 'That's definitely not how I want to be', but when you become the spectator in life, you are doing absolutely nothing towards discovering your Purpose.

Light from the candle shines on

"The purpose of morality is to teach you, not to suffer and die, but to enjoy yourself and live."

Ayn Rand

Life is about choices, and it's about *doing*. No sports athlete ever won a championship, or a game for that matter, by sitting on the sidelines. Yes, some people stay on the sidelines and go home with the trophies because their teammates won the game without them, but they didn't win it. Their teammates did.

When you coast through life without making any real effort, without trying to make something work out for you, then you are not burning much of a candle for yourself. Your light is too dim to make a difference, not only to other people but in the world as well.

We all know these people, the ones whose candle is barely flickering. They are the ones who live at home, with their parents still when they're into their thirties, who go to work at the supermarket to stock shelves because they don't want to make any real effort at anything. All they want to do is make enough money to buy the latest video game, computer console, or to go out to the local bar with their friends.

These people haven't invested in life and they are not the only ones, either.

Housewives whose children are all grown up, or who don't even have children or hire nannies to take care of them, and all they do is go to the local café to hang out with their friends, go shopping, or spend time at a spa are no different. These people don't have much ambition in life and lacking ambition is a dangerous thing. It's also contagious.

Spend time with someone who doesn't have any real desire to work or make an effort with anything that they do in life, and you will find that it is contagious. The people whom we surround ourselves with are often the same people whom we become.

Look at a couple that has been together for years, with one of them about a foot taller than the other. You'll notice that the taller person's shoulders droop and their head hangs lower. This is because of the height difference and they are used to bending down for the other person.

When you hang around with people who are lazy, who are unmotivated to do much of anything, then you tend to become the same way; you tend to become lazy and unmotivated yourself.

You may spend a considerable amount of time and energy focused on keeping yourself motivated and working hard, but the other person begins to act like dead weight, dragging you down.

If you have ever tried to swim in a lake with your clothes on, then you know the feeling of dead weight. It's an expression that is widely used, but many people have never actually experienced the sensation and how it can wear you down and begin to pull you under the surface of the water. When you are wearing your clothing, walking around on dry land, it feels normal; it feels natural. You have been doing this for the better part of your life, so it simply doesn't feel uncomfortable, or weighty.

However, if you were to jump into a lake with all of those clothes, the jeans, the sweatshirt, the sneakers and the socks, they absorb water and retain it. Suddenly those few simple pounds of clothing weigh ten or twenty pounds more. They begin to pull you down, even as you fight to keep your head above water. Your arms grow tired, as do your legs.

You are spending more energy just trying to stay afloat and you have less energy to actually swim towards the shore, towards the safe dry land.

Being around people who are lazy, especially when you are attempting to become motivated and live a full and meaningful life, is similar to trying to swim wearing all of your clothing. Those people are anchors around you and every moment that you spend surrounded by them, you are less likely to find the energy and courage to go out and do the things that you want to do.

Yet the more you are surrounded by these types of people, the heavier the burden because you grow tired. Just trying to stay 'afloat' in your life when others are doing nothing drains your energy and as you realize that you are not making any progress to get closer to the shore, you gradually give up and let the waters take you under.

When you are surrounded by people who are not motivated and are not making the effort to improve their own life, when they are not searching for their Purpose in life, have no relationship with God, or have nothing much going for them, then it forces you to burn your candle hotter just to keep moving through each day.

Finding the right balance

> *"When you dance, your purpose is not to get to a certain place on the floor. It's to enjoy each step along the way."*
>
> **Wayne Dyer**

Life is about finding balance. This is true whether you are searching for your Purpose or simply trying to get ahead at your job. Everything in nature, throughout the Earth and the universe is held in balance.

When you are burning through your candle too fast or when you are burning it too hot or at both ends, then your life is not in balance.

When your candle is barely flickering, then there is a lack of balance there as well. When it is burning too dim, then it makes it very difficult, sometimes impossible, to see the life around you. When it is burning to hot, then the brightness from the flame can drown out any other light or messages that you are seeking.

Life is about balance. God blessed your life with balance when you were born. Hopefully, as you grew up, you were given a fair balance from your parents, siblings, friends, and others who surrounded your life. The more years that pass, the more opportunity there is for our lives to fall out of balance.

We can meet the wrong people for us. We could find the wrong job and begin to spend too much time at that job. We could get married, have children, have our spouse leave us to raise the children alone, and then feel as though there is no time for anything else in our life.

In every moment within our life, God intended us to have balance and when we are not balanced, we are not burning our candle at the right amount. Thus, we are not able to connect with our Purpose, and we are not able to connect with God in the right way.

People make all kinds of arguments and excuses why they can't have balance. Bills, children need to get here or there, friends have left them stranded, debt, and the list will go on and on.

Excuses are easy. In fact, excuses are the easiest thing in the world to create. It doesn't take much ingenuity to devise excuses of why our lives are not in balance, or why we can't bring them into balance.

The difficult part is accepting that balance is vital to finding Purpose in your life, and that sometimes, if you truly want to find balance in your life, then you have to make sacrifices.

The sacrifices you make to bring your life into balance are often small ones such as asking for a little help with the children, which may mean swallowing your pride. Downsizing your home to pay less in rent, or a mortgage. Getting rid of the brand new SUV and buying a ten-year-old minivan instead.

If you are sitting around while someone else provides for you, and you're unmotivated to do anything, then the small sacrifices could include starting out with ten to twenty minutes a day devoted to helping a neighbour with some simple tasks. May be volunteering at a local shelter, or Picking up a hobby that you once enjoyed but gave up on years ago and make your life a bit productive.

Small sacrifices for a healthier and more balanced life can be the best start. You will find that once your life is in balance, then your candle will be lit properly and your Purpose will come into clearer focus.

Your Turn

Are you burning your candle at both ends? Or are you taking advantage of those around you and barely letting your candle flicker? Life isn't about the things that we possess or surround ourselves with; it's about the connections and the efforts that we make to and with those around us. If you are wearing yourself out, ask yourself why you're doing it? Even if it's for your children, what kind of message are you sending them? If it's because you want the 'better' life, then what kind of life might that be and when will you live it?

Sometimes life is best when it is simplified. When it is simplified, then many other things that you have been missing begin to come into focus.

CHAPTER 7

Burying the Past

"Everything in the universe has a purpose. Indeed, the invisible intelligence that flows through everything in a purposeful fashion is also flowing through you."

Wayne Dyer

Don't look now, but you're a product of your experiences, of your past. You may not feel that way at the moment, but the truth lies in everything that you do. You are what you have done throughout your life.

You are the end result of every moment that has passed in your life. Most of these moments have been long forgotten, so trivial at the time that we don't think much about them and our memories simply ignore them, but they helped to shape small pieces of who we have become.

When God smiled down on you and created you in His image, He knew that the work wasn't complete. He knew that you still have to form and shape the mold into the person you are now. He also knows that from this point in your life forward, you will continue to mold and shape and alter who you are.

His goal for you, though, has always been the same. The Purpose for your life has never changed, even though, through your experiences, you have changed.

Some of the events in our lives alter us in immensely positive ways, which brings us closer and closer to the person we were meant to become. Other events had negative impacts on us and they pull us away from who we were meant to be.

It is these negative events, too, that tend to stay with us far longer throughout our lives than the positive ones. The negative events in our lives shape us often far more than the positive ones and they begin to instill fear and apprehension within us that mold the course that we take into the future.

Our past is made up of millions of events that have had an impact on us. The negative ones can seem harmless to us when we look back on them, but they had an influence at the time and likely still do.

Do you recall being scolded for something that you didn't do? How did that make you feel? When you're a child, adults in your life are the authorities, they are the people whom you look to with reverence and as role models who seem to know everything. So when they punished you as a child for something you didn't do, you felt slighted, you felt persecuted, and you wondered what you could have done differently to convince them that you weren't the one responsible for it.

Have you ever lost a loved one to an illness or accident? As the elderly people in our life become sick, death is something we begin to expect, but when someone young and full of life passes suddenly, especially if it's someone to whom we were very close; it can leave an enormous void in our life.

Have you ever lost the love of someone whom you thought would be there with you until the end of time? Have you ever been cheated on? Have you been called names, taunted and teased, or even ridiculed by people you thought were your friends?

Negative events are all around us and it is those events that pull us away from our Purpose.

Think about a relationship that you had, whether it was with a boyfriend, girlfriend, spouse, or best friend at some time in your life that went sour. Whatever happened might have affected you for the rest of your life.

Someone who wakes up one day to realize that their loved one, their husband or wife has been cheating on them, will become less trusting and less willing to open up their heart to anyone else in the future.

A person whose best friend betrayed their confidence is likely to trust people less in the future.

A person who owns a store and is robbed at night is more likely to buy security systems for their business and their home and they will begin to tighten the reins on their children, their spouse, and others in the hope of keeping them safe.

A person whose neighbour is the victim of a violent crime might do the same thing.

We are shaped by these negative events and they often lead us to becoming more closed off, more isolated from everyone around us. God never intended you to shy away from people, or to hide from life, but the fear that we carry with us from these negative events in the past often make us do just that.

Letting go

> *"The devil can cite Scripture for his purpose."*
>
> **William Shakespeare**

One of the most difficult challenges that anyone faces in life is letting go of the past. We hold onto our past, not because we miss it, or long for the good old days, but because we are afraid of the unknown future that awaits us.

The past is known even though it may not be comfortable sometimes especially when it is considered negative. We know what happened, we know the result, and we know that we made it through, with our wounds and scars and all.

The future is a much different place altogether. The future is a vast expanse of possibilities and that often terrifies us. Even when we plan and build towards our future with all of the tools that God has bestowed us with, even when we calculate all of the variables and possibilities that line the path in front of us, we are still fearful because all around us, whether it's with our friends and relatives or subjects in the news, we see the bad things that happen to good people.

And this is often aided by our negative past events. We like to hold onto these negative past events because they remind us that we did indeed go through it and that, in order to avoid repeating the same mistakes, it's important for us to remember them, remember the events that led up to it, and do whatever we can to avoid the same thing happening all over again.

Because we don't want to live through that pain again, do we?

Events around the world or right next door will often remind us of those little things. People who lost loved ones will often say, "I can't believe he's gone," or "I'm never going to fill this void in my heart." They remind those who went through it how tough it was and how much they don't want to go through it again.

If someone lost a loved one to a car accident, they might make sure that their own children, when it's time for them to drive, take it seriously. They may delay giving them the right to drive, that privilege. These people may even stop driving themselves, too afraid of what might happen.

If you have ever driven on a wet, slick road, or on an icy patch of road, and skidded, even if you didn't crash, you must have slowed down for quite some time. Your nerves held you in check.

Sometimes these negative events in our lives are good things. Sometimes they keep us safe, especially if we were reckless in our youth.

Most of the time, however, these negative events keep us from moving forward, or they keep us from living life the way God intended us to. These negative events put chains around us and whenever we are in chains, we are not free.

Even though God granted us this wonderful freedom of life, we don't take advantage of it completely because we fear the unknown of the future.

Have you ever stopped to wonder why the past, even with all the hardship and negative events that each of us has faced, always warms us more than the future? It's because we know the result. Good or bad, we know what happened to us and it seems so much simpler than an unknown future.

While memories are wonderful things, and they are important to hold onto, there is a difference between remembering the past and being stuck in it.

If you don't do things today that you once enjoyed, or that you wished you could do, it's likely because of something in the past. It is the past that is holding you back from living your wonderful future.

It's time to stop and grab a shovel, dig the past a nice grave, and have a ceremony for it, and then finally bury it.

This doesn't mean that you have to forget about the past, or to negate that it ever happened. It means that you simply have to bury it away and accept that it did indeed happen, but that you made it through and it won't keep you from living your life any more.

God granted you Free Will. You can choose to remain trapped in the past, holding onto it because you think it makes you comfortable, or you can choose to bury the past, to let it go, and head out into your future with wide open arms and a hope that most adults long forget about once the negative events begin to pile up all around you.

Every passing moment is another opportunity to turn it all around.

When you bury your past, when you honestly bury your past, you do so with a willingness to accept whatever the future holds and has coming your way. You accept that not everything is going to work out smoothly and that tough times and tough losses are a part of life but still good things happen.

When you can do this, you open up all of the doors that you unwittingly closed along your path through life. When you open up all those doors, your Purpose in life will be there waiting for you once again.

If you can't bury your past, if you can't let things go, then you are probable to have a difficult time, if not an impossible time, finding your Purpose in life.

Being unable to bury the past means that you are stuck in it. God does not want you to be stuck in your past; He wants you to have your eyes wide open and looking to the future and living in the present.

As some people say, the future is unknown, the past is known, but the present is a gift and that's why it's called a present.

You are here for a reason and that reason is glorious. If you have trouble burying your past where it belongs, then there are people who can help. From counsellors to therapists to spiritual guidance, they surround us just about everywhere we turn.

There is no shame in seeking outside help for our troubles. There are many times when we think that we moved beyond our past, only to realize years later that we, in fact, only hid it in a corner of our heart. When that happens, it's still there, still influencing our life.

Some people believe that burying their past means tucking it away somewhere in their heart or their mind. Burying your past means that you accept what happened, that you will not let it stop you from living, and that you are ready and willing to move on to your wonderful future.

Your Turn

Is there something in your past that is keeping you from doing things in your life that you always wanted to do? Maybe you wanted to cook, but your grandmother—who was your inspiration in the kitchen—passed away too soon and every time you step into the kitchen, your heart aches because of that loss.

Everyone has tragedy, loss, and pain in their past. These are tests that God has given to us. Sometimes we are able to pass them, other times we don't, but no matter what happened, if we allow it to influence our life moving forward, then we slide away from the road we should be traveling down. We risk losing our Purpose.

Think about the events that have shaped you, think about their impacts as well and decide if you are able to bury them once and for all. If you can't, then consider speaking to a professional to help you work through the emotions that are tied to the events. This will often help to set you free.

CHAPTER 8

Building Bonds

"Let there be no purpose in friendship save the deepening of the spirit."

Kahlil Gibran

Have you ever heard of the expression, 'No man is an island'? There is more truth to that statement than in almost any other that has to do with the bonds that we create throughout our life.

When God created the earth and the heavens and then created man in His image, He didn't create just one person and He didn't intend for us to travel through life alone.

Humans are social creatures; we are meant to be surrounded by other people, to create bonds with other individuals. Some of these people with whom we share our life will have the same interests as we do while others will be completely different.

Too often, life gets in the way and we forget that building bonds is a conscious effort and one that we need to continually make every year of our life.

Take a moment to look around you and the people who are a part of your life. What kind of bonds do you share with these individuals? Are they even bonds or are they simply connections? Connections are one thing, bonds are completely different.

Friends with whom you talk maybe once in a while, whom you only see when you're at a school function for your children, or whom you might say hello to when you meet each other while out shopping for groceries aren't bonds. They are connections.

High school friends whom you've found on Facebook or another social networking site after ten or fifteen years are not bonds, they are connections.

An ex-husband or ex-wife with whom you only speak because you have a child together is not a bond, it's a connection.

A bond is formed when someone shares your life, in whatever capacity you're willing to share it. A bond is the kind of connection with a person who is there for you when you need them most, who knows your strengths and your weaknesses, your hopes and your fears.

A bond is formed when you invite this other person into your life without reservation.

We often wear masks to hide the real 'us' from other people, but God didn't intend us to wear masks, otherwise He would have given us some way to naturally hide ourselves from others. God wanted us to be open and honest with the people who surround our lives.

Most of the time we can determine who is a connection in our life as opposed to who is a bond by assessing the masks that we put on for them.

If you think of someone in your life whom you feel somewhat close to, do you hide some aspects of yourself from them? If so, they are not a true bond, but a connection and some friendships are fake.

If you think of someone in your life whom you would like to have a bond with, but know that it's only a connection, then what is it about yourself that you are keeping from them? Or are they keeping themselves from you?

Forming bonds with other people is a two-way street. It requires us to take steps into an unknown realm, to take chances and to allow ourselves to be exposed to potential pain. This is one of the main reasons why people don't form many bonds in their life, because they fear the potential pain that could come from that bond.

When we are children, we often form many bonds. We bond with people we barely know because we have few fears. As children, we haven't been exposed to the cruelty of other people yet. We are trusting and because of that trust, we are willing to share our lives with these other people without reservation.

As adults, we are much more guarded because we simply don't want to live through the same level of pain that we may have experienced at some time in our lives because most of us have been disappointed in one way or another. We feel content with only a few bonds and would rather leave the rest to connections.

Married couples with children might immediately assume that their spouse is a bond and that their children are bonds, but this is not true.

A bond is formed when two people share their lives equally and without censorship from one another, are willing to accept that there will be pain as well as joy and that one or both of them may inadvertently hurt the other through their words and actions, but that it would never be intentional.

People who share bonds with others in their lives don't need to see or talk to these people every day. They don't even need to speak to one another for months or even years to have a true bond. A bond is not about immediacy or physical closeness.

A bond is about the emotional context and the emotional connection. It is through bonds that we become closer to God and His intention for us and for our lives. Mathew 19:19 ". . . love thy neighbour as thyself" (KJV)

Recognizing connections

> *"In criticism I will be bold, and as sternly, absolutely just with friend and foe. From this purpose nothing shall turn me."*
>
> ### *Edgar Allan Poe*

Far too often people think of the connections in their life as bonds. The group of friends that you hang out with on the weekends may consist of some bonds, but they are more like connections if you never really share all of your life with them.

Do you tell these friends about the things that you desire most in life? Do you tell them, or would you be willing to tell them, about your dreams, your hopes and aspirations, even if they seem absolutely absurd to you? When one stops to consider these simple questions, the answer about whether they share a connection or a bond becomes clearer.

The defining characteristic of a bond is something that is forged. You don't forge a bond by simply hanging out with friends, sharing a few laughs, and maybe a drink or two.

Groups of friends that get together every day and stand up for one another through thick and thin are not necessarily bonds. Likely they are still only connections.

In your life, hopefully you have many friends and family members to whom you can turn when you feel lonely. But who would you be willing to share your most embarrassing thoughts or dreams or speculations? Is there anybody with whom you feel close enough to tell anything in the world?

Married couples often feel as though their 'bond' with their spouse is not as strong as they would like. Many women might report that they don't feel as though their husband understands them. They don't believe that they could share everything that they feel with their husbands.

Yet, at the same time, they love them with all of their heart and soul and the mere thought of losing him hurts too much to even consider.

Is this a bond? Or a connection? Think about it for a moment. Let's come back to that in a minute.

What about your children, if you have children? For those individuals who have older children, adult children, do you believe that they feel they could tell you anything at all about themselves, about their life, their love, their hopes and dreams? Could you do the same? Do you have a bond with your children or only a connection?

What about your relationship with God? Is it a connection or a bond? Do you share your innermost secrets with God? Of course you do. He knows everything about you, all of your thoughts and everything you do in your life, He knows all of it. But are you willingly sharing these things with Him? If not, then you are only connecting at a certain level with Him.

If you don't feel as though you could tell a person everything and anything about you, about your thoughts, or the dreams that you had, then you have a connection, not a bond.

Forming bonds requires a complete leap of faith with the other person. It doesn't mean that they will return the trust that you show to them. It only means that you are willing to bear your soul to them anytime that it is required.

How to form bonds

"The purpose of life is to be defeated by greater and greater things."

Rainer Maria Rilke

When you create bonds, the more bonds you make, the closer you become to everything and everyone around you. You become entwined with the energy of other living creatures and this brings you enlightenment and enrichment of your existence.

God does indeed have a plan for you, a Purpose, but He also intended you to not be alone in your journey through life. He intended you to share your life with others.

Your life is a gift and therefore, a gift is meant to be shared.

When you censor the things that you may feel embarrassed about, you are not allowing yourself to forge the bonds that illuminate life.

There may be things that you always thought about doing with your life, but somewhere along your road through it, you heard some people mention how silly it is, or how juvenile, or what a waste of time it would be and you decided from that moment on to keep it locked away.

When you did that, you shut out the prospect of bonds in the future.

People who will laugh at the things you might say are not people with whom you should forge bonds. You may like them, you may enjoy their company, but they may not be the type of people who will help you reach and discover your Purpose.

If you want to form bonds with other people, then you must be willing to listen to their thoughts, aspirations and dreams at the same time that you are willing to share yours. Bonds created are done so with a two-way street.

Many relationships tend to be one-directional, with one person dictating the boundaries and the rules and the expectations of that relationship. These are connections.

In order to form strong bonds with others, you need to speak up, to let the other person know that it's important to share these innermost feelings and emotions with them when and if you feel the need to do so.

Start by forming bonds with the people already closest to you such as your spouse, your children, your parents, or siblings. Begin to open up and tell them things that you might not have told them otherwise.

When we grow up and enter the 'real' world of working and raising a family, we tend to put away those smaller dreams and ambitions of our youth in the name of being responsible, yet often the things that we longed to do or to be when we were younger were closer to our true Purpose than where we end up.

When we forge strong bonds and begin to share all of these inner emotions and ideas and hopes, then we begin to bring back that instinct that God gave us.

He gave us a Purpose when we were created and it is imprinted on our soul. The noise of life can drown it out, but through time, through strong bonds and not simple connections, we can have the strength and the energy that is required to hear it once again.

When you have bonds in your life, everything seems possible. When you only have connections, you feel alone.

Forge bonds from the connections that you have at the moment. Strengthen bonds that already exist.

By doing so, you will be that much closer to finding your Purpose in life.

Your Turn

How many bonds do you think you have in your life right now? Name
the people who you feel you have a true bond with:

_____

_____

_____

_____

_____

_____

_____

_____

_____

Of these people, would you share your innermost secret with? Would you
tell them anything? What about the embarrassing thought or dream that
you might have had one night? If you would, then do it. Call them up and
tell them. If you can't, then your bond is not as strong as you thought.

CHAPTER 9

Ready to Serve

"Preparation for old age should begin not later than one's teens. A life which is empty of purpose until 65 will not suddenly become filled on retirement."

Dwight L. Moody

When you go to work at your job, you are serving a master. You are serving some higher power. Even if you own your own business, you are serving those that pay your bills: your customers.

Service has received a bad reputation in recent years, mostly because the idea of being a servant has been equated to being a slave, though that is far from reality.

Serving . . . truly and honestly serving . . . is about love, not slavery. When you serve someone, you do it out of the kindness of your heart, you do it because you want to show your love and appreciation and support to the person whom you are serving.

The word 'serve' has been related to many other acts throughout life that it has lost its true and fundamental meaning. Some of the terms that the word serve has become too closely associated with in recent years include:

- The waitress served the meal to the diners.
- The politician served his people.
- I was served papers to appear in court.
- Mom said, "Dinner is served."
- Service with a smile.
- Customer service because we care.

The word serve, or service, has become a tag line in marketing and advertising. It is associated too often with acts or deeds that are *required* of people.

This leads one to believe, and often rightly so, that service is not something that one does out of love or desire, but out of necessity. When was the last time you went to a restaurant and found the service to be openly and honestly warm and inviting? As though the waiter or waitress was actually doing their passion, rather than fulfilling the obligations of their job? A service at restaurants is an obvious example because the pay tends to be low and as a result, the service tends to reflect this.

Go to a five-star restaurant or hotel and you are likely to see their services appearing to be from the heart however, in reality, the jobs are so competitive to get, so the waiters and waitresses put on a great show. In most cases, it's all an act.

Most people, who work, don't really have much passion or desire to do what they're doing; they basically work through the motions without much of a care about it. Sure, they serve their bosses or their customers, and sometimes they even know the right things that they're supposed to say (many businesses now have scripts that their employees are supposed to read to their customers to make sure that the customers feels as though their business is honestly appreciated) but in their heart, they are only doing it for a paycheck.

They are doing it for a reward.

True service doesn't expect a reward at the end of the service. True service is done because of that inner love, that inner sense of purpose.

The waitress who rushes the food to the customers, who continually checks up to make sure that they have everything they need, who is there with a smile even when things go wrong, or when the order is mistaken, doesn't do all of that because she's in a good mood. She does it because she believes, and has been taught for most of her life, that customers will reward her with generous tips if she is friendly and her service is exceptional.

Go to a diner or restaurant and watch how the waiting staff act and react to different types of tippers. People who tip generously, when they return are often greeted warmly. Those who are stingy or don't leave any tip tend to be ignored, for the most part.

If you want to serve God, then the question that you should answer is why? Why do you want to serve God? Do you believe that, through your service to Him, you are going to be welcomed into the warm embrace of heaven? Do you believe that eternal glory will be yours if you serve Him here?

What is truly in your heart when you offer your service to God? Remember, you can't hide what's in your heart from God. He knows what you think and He knows what you do. And He will know if your service is being provided out of a sense of duty, a desire for reward, or out of love.

Of course, serving God doesn't just revolve around doing acts for Him, spreading His word, or even going to church every week. Serving God is about serving your Purpose.

When you know your Purpose in life, and you have the open and honest desire to fulfill that Purpose, then you are serving God, yourself and all of your loved ones.

Serving your Purpose sometimes means making major life changes. You may discover that what you are here to do, your Purpose in this life, can't be done where you are at the moment. You may find that you have to move thousands of miles away to fulfill your Purpose.

If you realize that a major life change is required of you for your service, and you accept it grudgingly, then you are not honestly serving your Purpose. You are not doing it out of love, but out of a sense of obligation. You are doing it because you expect some kind of reward in the end.

Serving one step at a time

"Definiteness of purpose is the starting point of all achievement."

W. Clement Stone

Rome wasn't built in a day. Neither was the Great Wall of China. When you are searching for your Purpose in this life, you will be required to take many small steps, placing one stone on top of another for some time before you finally achieve your true Purpose.

A journey of a thousand miles begins with one step. When you serve God, your Purpose, or someone else, the process can take a considerable amount of time to build, develop, and get used to. For some people, they understand that their Purpose has already been known and they have been working towards it for most of their life.

These people may be rewarded for their work. Doctors are often called to their profession. They may feel drawn to the idea of helping people when they are ill, healing them, and assisting them on their way to recovery. To become a doctor, an individual must spend many years in school studying and taking tests.

Some doctors have only gone into the profession because they were after the large paychecks. The ones that felt the true desire to help will likely find that they are financially set for life with their jobs. They might drive the nice cars, live in beautiful homes, and go to fancy parties.

Yet this doesn't detract from their service, because they would still do what they are doing even if they were being paid minimum wage.

Some people might snicker at that notion, having bad experiences with doctors and medical care professionals, but these people do exist and they would honestly continue in their profession if the money disappeared. That is true passion for their Purpose.

Those people know what they were meant to do with their life. They took their service one step at a time, though most of their adult friends and the people whom they surround themselves with once they are doctors invested in their profession never saw those first steps. They took those first steps when they were children, when they first knew what they were meant to do and they never regretted the decision.

Sure, they might have had their doubts at times, wondering if they would have been better as musicians or lawyers or business executives, but in their heart, they knew and still know what they are here to do. And whether they believe in God or not, they are still serving Him and they are doing it with love.

As an adult, when you find your Purpose in life, and if it requires you to change, meaning you aren't fulfilling your Purpose at this time, then you will need to make some changes. You will need to take some small steps to move you in that direction.

You shouldn't make drastic changes at first, because if you do, then you may become overwhelmed with stress and pressure and that could once again lead you off the path to your true Purpose.

As an adult, you have many insecurities and fears that have followed you. Even when you successfully bury your past, you will still have the residual emotions that were tied to those events. You need to overcome some of your fears and your apprehensions and talk about your new Purpose with those individuals with whom you've developed strong bonds.

Clarity of all of your decisions is critical to the process of following your heart's desire, which ultimately is God's imprint on your soul about your Purpose.

People often will turn to prayer to help them make these first tender steps into their brave new world. Praying for God's guidance can help soothe those fears that you have and come across.

If your Purpose demands that you change careers, or locations, then take these first small steps:

- Find out what degree you might need from a university if necessary.
- Determine where you might need to move to.
- If you are to help children through teaching, what credentials would you need?
- If you want to open your own business, how do you start?
  - What does your town require for permits?
  - How many employees would you need?
  - How much money will you need to get started?

- Find the support of your friends and family (it may require some time and convincing on your part, but those are the small steps that are important as you begin your journey to serve and into your purpose)

When you're ready to serve, you will know it. Taking the steps that have already been presented in this book will lead you to the path on which your true Purpose lies. However, it is such a bad thing if you know what to do and you don't do it. You are doing yourself a disservice. You might never stop asking yourself questions about life if you don't know what you are here for.

The idea of change is often frightening because of the unknown, but what tends to startle people or cause them to give up on their Purpose, or their passions in life, is that they attempt to make too many drastic changes.

They try to take on too much too quickly. God understands that your life has been built around you and that sometimes change requires you to unravel from all of the chaos and even good intentions that others provide for you.

That's why being ready to serve doesn't mean that you're ready to jump into the raging waters. First you need to learn how to swim. Then you need to put on some safety gears. Then maybe you need to take a few lessons on navigating through the rough seas.

Being prepared to serve is about heading into your new life with care. If you take small steps, even if you don't reach your Purpose for many years, every little step you take, even if it's the simple process of building up your thoughts and your courage, are actually serving your Purpose and for that, you will be serving God.

Life is all about small steps. When you're ready to take yours, then you are ready to serve.

Your Turn

Have you determined what your Purpose is in life? It's okay if you don't. Even trying to discover it are the first few steps. Just picking up this book means that you have already taken some of those first steps and for that, congratulations. It should make you feel wonderful to be pursuing your Purpose and trying to strip away the clutter that has clouded it from your view all these years.

If you have discovered your Purpose or you are still searching, list the next few steps that you will need to take in order to fully serve it.

_____

_____

_____

_____

_____

_____

_____

_____

_____

CHAPTER 10

Acquiring Weapons for Life

"When freedom does not have a purpose, when it does not wish to know anything about the rule of law engraved in the hearts of men and women, when it does not listen to the voice of conscience, it turns against humanity and society."

Pope John Paul II

You have been blessed with one of the most important weapons for life and it came to you from birth. It is called Free Will.

God granted you this immensely powerful weapon of Free Will, but for many it has caused them to stray from the path that they were destined to follow.

The beauty of Free Will, though, also comes with a great responsibility. With Free Will, you can't simply say that something is impossible for you to do.

You can't rely on the easy road out. In fact, you can't expect to find your Purpose and then refuse to follow by saying that it's just not possible.

Far too many people fall back on the standard excuses of, 'I have a family, there's nothing I can do about my Purpose.'

Or, even, 'I'm a parent. My purpose is to raise my children and that's what I'm going to do.'

Great, wonderful. You're a parent and your devotion to them is perfect. Yet it is not your Purpose in life. It is not the grand design that God had in mind for you. Just about everyone on Earth can have children; it's not a destiny. Whether you have one, two, or ten or more children, it doesn't absolve you from finding your Purpose and living to achieve it.

Your free will allows you the luxury of choosing to not follow your Purpose because you are either too scared of the unknown or you think that it is simply too difficult to do.

Free will also gives you the power to say to yourself that no matter what anyone else says or does, it is entirely up to you whether you find your Purpose and whether you follow through to serve your Purpose.

You may say that your husband won't allow you to quit your job as an accountant to pursue your Purpose of being a teacher to young children.

Why not?

Does he have you chained to your house? Does he force you into a cage every day when you get home from work?

If he did, then you would have an argument that you don't have true free will, but in most cases, this doesn't happen. Some spouses or family members may ridicule you for what you have found as your passion. Some may espouse you in considering carefully what you're thinking about doing. Some may tell you that they will leave you if you do this thing that you want to do.

That's their choice. That's *their* free will. Yours is to allow them to bully you into submission or to find a way to convince them that this Purpose is your passion and the reason that you were sent to this Earth, the reason that you were given life.

Of course, Free Will is not the only weapon that God has given you in your task of fulfilling your Purpose.

Some people find that they have talents that can make them a lot of money and they use their talents to do so, not realizing that those very talents were likely placed upon them by God for something completely different.

There are countless musicians throughout the world who have uncanny abilities and have made millions of dollars using those talents, but they don't serve their Purpose. There are a few who do fulfill their Purpose and still make a lot of money. The difference between these two types are the ones that use their talents to become rich and in turn ignore their Purpose end up feeling empty in the end.

When the days of their life become short, they begin to look back on the retrospective of their choices and find something inherently missing from it.

They feel lost and alone. Regardless of how many people surround them at the end of their days, they still feel alone.

Other weapons to use

> *"I know in my heart that man is good. That what is right will always eventually triumph. And there's purpose and worth to each and every life."*
>
> **Ronald Reagan**

It's important not to think of weapons as being destructive. When we talk about arming yourself with the right weapons for your life, we are not referring to going into battle to inflict harm on others, but rather to find your way through the dense brush of life.

A machete is a weapon that can be used in battle, but it can also be used to cut down brush in the woods to help you reach your destination. Think of weapons in this manner.

Remember, it's your choice how you use them, because God granted you Free Will.

Some of the other weapons that you have been given to help you in your pursuit of your Purpose include:

- Intelligence
- Special talents

These can include:

- Science
- Music
- Art
- Modeling

- Acting
- Mathematics
- Writing
- Repairing things
- Teaching
- And much more
- Reason
- Language
- Desire
- Motivation
- And more

These may not seem like weapons in an arsenal for life, but they are essential to success, no matter who uses them or who chooses not to use them.

Everyone has a special talent. It doesn't matter whether you have an IQ to match Einstein's, whether you run the mile faster than anyone has ever run it, whether you're in a wheelchair, or whether you can't figure out how to add two plus two; everyone has a talent.

There is something you do, and likely many things that you do though you choose not to recognize it, that sets you apart from other people. I could write a list of thousands of possibilities of talents that you may possess and all I would do would be to waste several pages.

You need to look within yourself to determine what it is that you do well, or that you have a natural gift for. It doesn't mean that you have to be good at something right now to have talent.

Michael Jordan is considered one of the greatest basketball players in history, but even with all of his talent, when he started playing, he is likely to have missed more shots than he made.

Everyone has to begin somewhere, but your talent was given to you as a weapon in your pursuit of fulfilling your Purpose.

You have a brain and can reason through problems. In other words, you can problem solve and that means that anything that you need or want to do with your life can be done. Sometimes you have to work through the situation first, find the best solution, and then make a plan that will help you achieve that end.

You were blessed with the gift of language and reason. Even if you don't have the ability to speak, you can communicate through other means. We are taught the basics of language when we are young. We use language to tell others what we want to do.

We have reasoning abilities so that we can determine if something we plan on doing will work, or whether we need to consider a different course of action.

Perhaps one of the most important weapons that we have in life to help us with our Purpose is desire and motivation. These are also some of the most elusive weapons and most fleeting.

We can lose our desire and motivation within a blink of an eye. Things don't always work out the way that we hoped, or planned, and for some, that is enough to cause them to stop what they're doing, to give up, pack it in, and try to leave it all behind in the past.

God granted you desire and motivation to help you through the darkest of nights, not to give up when things get tough. Remember, when things are difficult, they are a challenge from God. They are God's way of testing you and helping to teach you the important lessons that you will need at some later time when the going gets really rough.

As easy as desire is to lose, as easy as it is to lose motivation, getting them back can be exponentially difficult. Everyone loses desire and motivation from time to time. The key is to dig deep within yourself, find it again, and reignite the flame. Without desire or motivation, you will not be able to capture and successfully fulfill your Purpose.

These weapons that you have been given by God have all been handed to you in order for you to live a life of Purpose.

Love them. Embrace them. Hold them close. And if you've lost them, or feel as though you've lost them, know that He didn't give you something that you could lose.

His gifts are forever and all you have to do is look for them and you will find them.

Your Turn

Can you identify the weapons that you have been given to by God? Everyone has several. Some have more than others, depending on their Purpose.

Write down as many of the weapons that you possess, whether they are honed or dormant, and also indicate whether you believe that you can maximize them to their greatest intent. If you find that some are not ideal for you, then you may soon realize that your Purpose will not be completely fulfilled so be honest with yourself.

_____

_____

_____

_____

_____

_____

_____

_____

CHAPTER 11

Secrets to Finding Success

"We should not look back unless it is to derive useful lessons from past errors, and for the purpose of profiting by dearly bought experience."

George Washington

One of the most basic and common questions that people have in life is how does one find success?

We look around everyday and see people who have found success, but then if we get the chance to speak to these individuals, we learn that they don't feel as though they have been as successful as they seem to us. The grass always seems to be greener on the other side of the fence.

If you have never heard that expression, it's an important one. If you have, then you know what it refers to. When someone says that the grass is always greener on the other side, they are referring to the idea that when we look at another person's life, their success, the things they have, it is easy to wish that their success and the things that they have were ours. Yet, if we get to that point in life where we attain those things, we may look at the life we once had, before all of that success and glory and material possessions that we earned, and wish that we had it back again.

Life can become complicated when we find a certain level of success. If you have been living your life for many years at a certain level, even if it's struggling to pay bills and make ends meet, then you may find that, once you have money to spare, that the hectic lifestyle and the pressure that comes with success is not something you counted on and long for the days when it was simpler, and more comfortable.

Everyone will define success differently. There is no way to get around that basic fact. You cannot ask one individual what the secret is to his or her success and turn around and apply it to everyone.

It all begins with what you define as being success.

Ask about one hundred people and you will likely find more than a few dozen answers on what defines success. Some of these answers could be:

- Having a happy and healthy family

- Having money

- Being able to go on vacations every year

- Being promoted at work

- Getting a diploma from a university

- Buying the fancy sports car

- Having the large house with a superb view

- And so many more

The way to find success in your own life is to first define what you would consider as success. As we have been moving through this book, we have talked about many of the misperceptions that befall people in modern society about what they are meant to do with their life, what God handed down as their Purpose.

To desire money is fine, but when it is the sole driving force for doing something, then it will only cloud your true meaning of life, the reason why you are here in the first place.

The desire for the promotion at work is fine, but if you will only consider yourself as successful because of that promotion, then you are clouded on your true Purpose. What happens if you work all of those hours, put in the time and energy to your job, even sacrificing spending quality time with your family, and never get that promotion?

Or what happens several months after you attain that promotion? Are you going to remain content with your success? Or will you then wish for even more? Another promotion? The next step?

Success in life isn't measured for a few months. You don't find true success in life and then several months later realize that you want more. That isn't true success.

True, honest success comes from within, not from without. Most people tend to measure their success *against* other people. They measure their success in terms of money, houses, cars, material possessions, the position they attain at work and all of the other superficial means that we have grown accustomed to throughout the years.

The secret to finding success is looking deep within yourself, within your own life, and within your heart and determining what is your Purpose in this life.

If you live your life to fulfill your Purpose, then you are going to find success every single time. You won't need to worry about what other people think about you. You won't need to try and make as much money as possible to have the nice, big house high on the hill or the fancy cars or the expensive jewellery.

When you find your Purpose, you will inherently find your success and it will be a beautiful thing because when you do this, you will be closer to God than at any other time in your life, and closer than you may have ever thought possible. After all, He gave you this Purpose and He is waiting for you to find it to fill your heart with all of the love and hope and success that you will ever need.

Find your Purpose and you will find your success

> *"The main purpose of life is to live rightly, think rightly, act rightly. The soul must languish when we give all our thought to the body."*
>
> **Mohandas Gandhi**

There is basically only one secret to success in life and that is to find your Purpose and live your life to fulfill that Purpose.

God gave you life. He gave you breath, a heart and a soul and the Earth to live on. He gave you family and loved ones with whom to share this amazing gift and all that He has ever asked of you in return is to live your life to fulfill the Purpose that He bestowed upon you.

There are many people who have found riches beyond their wildest dreams, whose success in the business world afforded them the luxuries that few of us will ever know. Yet, you may not realize this, but these people often find themselves working harder and harder with each passing year, searching to fill a void within themselves that they simply cannot fill.

They don't know why they feel empty. They look around their lives and see everything that they ever wanted. They have the mansions, the vacation homes in the resort communities around the world, the yachts and the fine art and family and friends that never seem to end, but they still don't feel complete.

It is likely that they never will feel complete. Ultimately, they don't know that they are missing the most important thing within their life. They don't know that they haven't lived their life to fulfill their Purpose.

Some people will have those riches and be completely content, though, because they have fulfilled their Purpose or are living their life to that end. These people would be content and satisfied even if they lost everything they had tomorrow, as long as they would be able to continue to fulfill their life's purpose.

So, my friend, the secret to finding success in your own life is to determine what it is that you are here for. Why did God give you this gift of life?

The journey to finding that answer is not always an easy one, but it is a rewarding one. You must take steps, small steps, to clear away all of the clutter that life has thrown in your path and which clouds the vision for your Purpose in life.

Every choice you make is completely yours, even when you feel that others control your destiny. No one has any true control over your life. Not even God.

He has a goal for you, He has a wish that he wants to see you fulfill, but He can't and won't force it upon you. He gave you a free will. Yet the promise of happiness rests at the end of the road to reach your Purpose and set your life on the right path.

You won't find easy answers during many of the crossroads that you will encounter on your journey through this life in pursuit of your Purpose. You won't find simplicity.

Often, your road will challenge you. You have been raised and taught that certain things in life are important, whether intentionally or coincidentally taught these things.

It will be up to you to determine what are the really important things in life and which are sugar coated fantasies designed to keep your Purpose hidden from you.

The secret to success rests within your heart and when you can clear away all of the clutter inside, you will find it. Success is not found in money. It is not found in possessions. It is not found in the number of friends you have. It is not found in children or family.

Success is right there within you. That may be the most beautiful thought of all, isn't it? To know that all you need in your life to be successful is already there within you.

My blessings to you and your eternal success.

> *"The wise man should restrain his senses like the crane and accomplish his purpose with due knowledge of his place, time and ability."*
>
> **Chanakya**

About Sharon Sydney Miranda

Sharon is a child of God, an Entrepreneur, Speaker, Author, and a Network Marketer.

Sharon is the CEO of Wealth Magnets Company. After understanding that the majority of people struggle financially because they lack financial education and also because they do not have the discipline to create wealth, Sharon started this company to work with individuals to improve not just their finances but their lives as well.

She runs two on line ministries. (Youth and Women Empowerment) She supports families in Africa by providing money for food and other necessities. Due to her experience with this, she has started the 'Sharon Sydney Miranda Foundation' to help fight hunger in Africa and around the world.

In this day and age, no person should go without food or clean drinking water and Sharon hopes to raise awareness of this continuing problem in Africa and other places in the world.

If you would like to become involved in the Miranda Foundation, or to donate money to help these impoverished families, please visit any of Sharon Miranda's websites for more information. The dates will be published when this project will be officially started so stay tuned.

The websites include:

www.MywealthMagnets.com

www.SharonMirandas.com

www.WomenEmpowermentSite.com

www.YouthEmpowermentSite.com

As we learn in life, any help is important help. As you seek your Purpose, may God bless you in all that you seek and all that you do in life.

Shalom!

Lightning Source UK Ltd.
Milton Keynes UK
29 March 2011

170088UK00001B/31/P